LISZT

HUNGARIAN RHAPSODY NO. 2 FOR THE PIANO

EDITED BY MAURICE HINSON

AN ALFRED MASTERWORK EDITION

Alfred

econd Edition

over art: Liszt at the Piano, *1840*
by Josef Danhauser (1804–1845)
Oil on wood. (48" x 63¾")
Nationalgalerie SMPK, Berlin
Archiv für Kunst und Geschichte, Berlin

FRANZ LISZT
Hungarian Rhapsody No. 2

Edited by Maurice Hinson

Foreword

Liszt composed nineteen *Hungarian Rhapsodies*, the first fifteen of which were published between 1851 and 1853, while the last four date from the 1880's. These *Hungarian Rhapsodies* belong to Liszt's paraphrases. Like Brahms and his *Hungarian Dances*, Liszt made use of "urban" folk music melodies; standing quite apart from the phenomenal peasant folklore of Hungary they have retained a freshness and charm in their own right. The *Hungarian Rhapsodies* are perfect creations of their own kind. The material Liszt uses in them could not have been treated with more genius and beauty. This treatment utilizes the principles of the gypsy style and heightens them to an infinite degree: roving freedom that makes free use of rubato (robbed time) and accelerando that yields a degree of expressiveness almost unknown before that time, romantic exaltation, curious modulations, volatility and abruptness, renunciation of all metrical strictness—all these elements awakened great feelings of congeniality in Liszt.

Liszt reported on the *Hungarian Rhapsodies* in his book *The Gypsies and Their Music in Hungary* of 1859. From this, it appears that he made large collections of these "gypsy" melodies and regarded them as constituting a central portion of Hungarian culture; he saw them as parts of a larger totality, parts that in their great variety of forms and types, could be viewed as corresponding to components of a great gypsy epic period. It is this conception that lies behind the term "rhapsody": the epic quality attributed to melodies and their texts. The *Hungarian Rhapsodies* were preceded by earlier versions under the title *Magyar Dallok* (*Hungarian National Melodies*) in ten books, the last six which bore the title *Magyar rhapsodiac* (*Hungarian Rhapsodies*), all published between 1840 and 1847.

When performing this piece, despite all the virtuosity it demands, mere technical bravura should never predominate.

About the Piece

The best-known of the *Hungarian Rhapsodies* is the No. 2 in C-sharp minor—a veritable textbook of Hungarian gypsy fire and passion.

The form of this piece (found also in the Rhapsodies Nos. 13 and 19) is based on the *Lassan-Friska* principle. This principle uses a binary form in which the slow, dreamy first section, revels in rubato and builds up tension, and is followed by a dancelike, joyously animated second section in which the tension is released.

This work, like all of the *Hungarian Rhapsodies*, is composed in sections differing in length, speed, and expressive style. The introduction (measures 1–8) should be rather free and capricious. Measure 9 introduces the *Lassan* (slow) section with its strong melody over a heavy accompaniment. The graceful and melancholy part of this section occurs in measures 27 forward and should be rhythmically more relaxed than the preceding eighteen bars. A new capricious mood is gradually introduced in measures 35–56 and evolves into a brief cadenza before the opening idea returns. The cadenza at measure 84 imitates a native Hungarian percussion instrument, the cimbalom, in its quick repetition of notes between the hands.

The *Friska* (fast) section begins at measure 118 and continues to the end. Measures 306 to the end have a strong suggestion of the circus; one can almost hear the crack of the ringmaster's whip, and almost see the equestrienne leaping through paper-covered hoops. Good wrists and forearm rotation are necessary.

This edition is dedicated with admiration and appreciation to Mark Wait, a superb pianist, who knows how to play Liszt without letting the notes get in the way of the music.

Maurice Hinson

About this Edition

All pedal markings in this edition are Liszt's. He uses the indication 𝆮 , and its cancellation by ✻. Our more modern instruments in places demand a more frequent change of pedal. The absence of a pedal sign must not be taken to mean *senza pedale* (without pedal). All fingerings in italic type are Liszt's, all in Roman type are the editor's suggestion. The *ossia* at measures 393–408 is Liszt's suggestion for a slightly easier version. The sign ʌ denotes a rather sharp accent, whereas the sign > merely affects dynamic emphasis.

Liszt's notation frequently departs from normal usage when he tries graphically to capture the methods of playing and the peculiar characteristics of popular gypsy bands. He frequently departed from the indicated time-signature within a bar in order to accommodate either more or fewer note values than are proper to the indicated unit. Sometimes even the note values notated in one hand fail to tally with those in the other hand.

The marking *a capriccio,* (indicated at measure one of this piece), as used by Liszt denotes metrical irregularity. Rhythmic and agogic signs, above all in slow sections, show how concerned Liszt was to indicate in notational terms every single nuance. In such passages one can almost see early attempts at notating Hungarian *Sprechgesang* (speechsong) that already point forward towards the notational innovations of later folkmusic researchers.

These sections contain numerous ornaments that are commonly found in gypsy band performances. Virtuoso cadenzas and strange sound effects—some of them suggesting stringed instruments, others the cimbalom (the native percussion instrument of Hungary), leave their imprint on Liszt's piano style in these works and clearly point up its orchestral character. Liszt sometimes used normal type for his ornaments and at other places used smaller type.

The Grove number is from *The New Grove Dictionary*, Vol. 11: Liszt's Works (Compiled by Humphrey Searle, London: Macmillan, 1980). The Raabe number comes from Dr. Felix Raabe: "Verzeichnis aller Werke Liszts" (from Peter Raabe's *Liszts Schaffen*, Tutzing: Schneider, 1968).

HUNGARIAN RHAPSODY NO. 2

(RHAPSODIE HONGROISE)

Franz Liszt (1811–1886)
Raabe 106, Grove 244

Composed in 1847, published in 1851.

ⓐ All fingerings in italics are Liszt's.

19
cresc.
sf
24
26
dolce con grazia
p
30
35
capriccioso
dolciss.
ten.

39
ten.
43
sempre pp e leggieriss.
Ped.
46
48
delicatamente
51
p sempre giocando

54
57
più dim.
pp
61
quasi cadenza
cresc. molto
62
come prima
f
67
rit.
ritenuto
espressivo assai

73
79
f
84
quasi cadenza
accelerando
sf
3 2 1 3 2 1 3 2 1 3 2 1 3
3 2 1 3 2 1 3 2 1 3 2 1 3
cresc. molto
rinforz.
dim.
85
espressivo
p dolce

90
95
sfz
dim.
più p
e
100
dim.
105
rit.
un poco
111
rallentando
marcato
morendo
lunga pausa

FRISKA

Vivace
118
pp
124
pp
Ped.
130
sempre pp
136
non tanto presto, capricciosamente
142

148
153
158
poco a poco accelerando e crescendo
163
168
Ped.

crescendo molto
173
Ped.
Ped.
Tempo giusto—vivace
178
f marcato assai
sempre staccato
Ped.
Ped.
Ped.
Ped.
185
piano scherzando
il basso sempre staccato
senza ped.
pp
192
p
pp
leggieriss.
p
Ped.
Ped.
Ped.
Più mosso
200
Ped.
Ped. sempre

205
210
pp
215
leggiero ma ben marcato
220
sim.
225
marcato

230
8
poco a poco accelerando il
sempre p
sempre stacc.
tempo
236
8
243
8
250
8
8
sf
sf
256
8
8
sf
sf

262
stringendo con strepito
8
268
8
ff
274
a tempo
fff brioso assai
sf
Ped.
280
8
tutta forza e prestezza
sempre Ped.
285
8

calmandosi poco a poco
290
8
di - - mi - - nu - - en - - do
295
accelerando
p
sempre stacc.
300
pp
Ped.
304
p ma ben marcato
sotto
sopra
pp senza ped.
309

314
p e sempre stacc.
320
sotto
sopra
326
p e sempre stacc.
332
8
338
8
cresc. molto
Ped.
Ped.
Ped.

344
stringendo
8
Ped.
350
rinforz.
355
rinforz.
361
a tempo
fff brioso assai
sf
Ped.
367
tutta forza
sempre Ped.

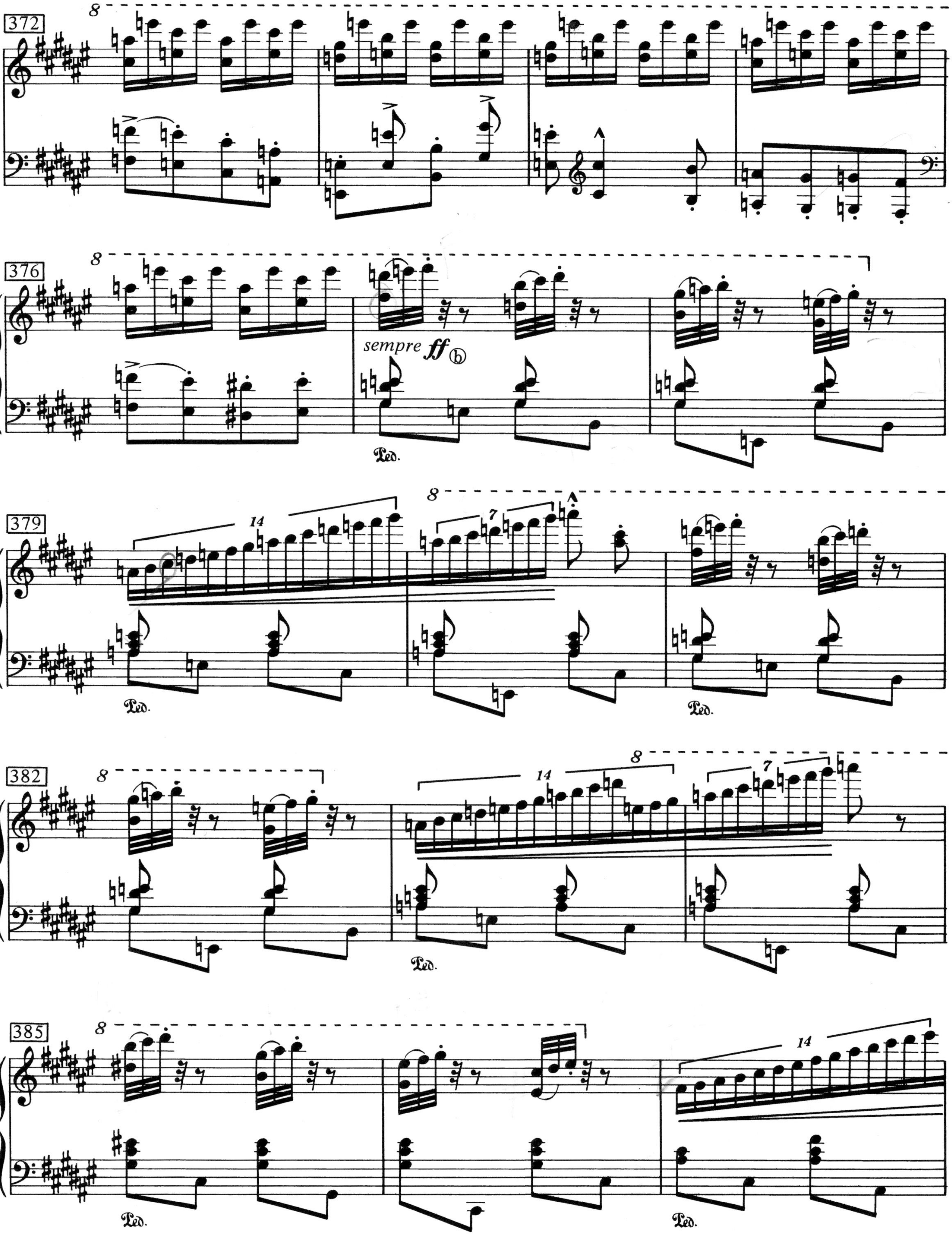

ⓑ In Liszt's autograph the ***ff*** is followed by the word *sfogato,* which means unrestrained, given free rein, let loose.

388
391
Ossia
poco a poco dim.
394
398
Ped.

© In 1885 Liszt wrote a whole series of cadenzas to this Rhapsody. The cadenza for this section is given below in two different versions.

Cadenza (Between measures 420 and 421) for Lina
sempre piano
Cadenza
(Between measures 420 and 421) for Tony Raab
pp
p
tr
2
Ped.
trillo (legato ed accelerando)
8
p
cre - - scen - do
molto
Ped.
8
4
ff
fff
3 2
2 3
sempre ped.
un poco rallentando
2 3
ten.
ten.
Ped.

421
Prestissimo
pp martellato
426
cresc.
Ped.
431
Ped.
più cresc.
Ped.
Ped.
8
436
8
ff
Ped.
Ped.
441
Ped.
Ped.
sf
Adagio
ff
Ped.
Presto
8

Alfred